Ricard & la Gastronomie Française

24 Recipes from Great French Chefs

The measurements used in this book are
American cups/tablespoons followed by metric
measures in parentheses.

Since American and British measures differ,
the table on page 46 will enable British users
to convert from either of these systems.

Since the begining of the century, Ricard has been using a formula combining anise, licorice and other aromatic plants to produce its famous "pastis" in the sunny south of France.

Mixed with water and ice, Ricard is a perfect thirst quencher. Once a local speciality, its popularity has spread far beyond its native France to become appreciated throughout the world.

This collection of 24 recipes was created for Ricard by some of the greatest chefs in France. Six famous chefs from 3-star restaurants in the Michelin Guide, each chose another talented though less renowned colleague to join him on this project. Each of the twelve created 2 recipes incorporating the unique and refreshing taste of Ricard.

Most of the chefs practice what has come to be known as "La Nouvelle Cuisine Française": they have created dishes in which the products used are of the highest quality, and in which light, subtly-flavored sauces abound.

For many years, chefs have known that Ricard and fish make a great combination. The following recipes demonstrate how perfectly Ricard can be used to make delicious meat and poultry dishes, as well as desserts.

Ricard and fine cooking have much in common; both contribute to the pleasure of living, or as the French would say, "la joie de vivre".

Claude Lebey

Near Lyon

Alain Chapel
La Mère Charles, Mionnay, (Ain).

Small red mullet with star anise and orange.

Pigeon pot-au-feu with star anise, fried
ravioli, and poached pigeon eggs.

Jacques Guy.
Le Petit Relais, Coligny, (Ain).

Corn crêpes with Ricard.

Brill fillets with shallot butter sauce.

Alain Chapel "La Mère Charles".

Alain Chapel was born in Lyon on December 30, 1937. Just before the last World War, his father, an experienced maître d'hôtel, bought a little bistrot in the town of Mionnay called La Mère Charles.

A naturally talented cook, Alain Chapel studied with Fernand Point before working with his father at La Mère Charles in 1967. The talents of this gifted chef were immediately appreciated by French food critics: by 1969 the restaurant merited two stars in the Michelin Guide, and in 1973 a third was awarded. The little bistrot became a famous establishment, a "must" for every gourmet visiting Lyon. There, a true artist, Alain Chapel prepares light and subtle dishes, full of poetry.

Small Red Mullet with Star Anise and Orange.

Tout petits rougets de Méditerranée infusés à l'anis.

Ingredients for 4 servings:
12 small red mullet weighing 1 ³/₄ oz (50 g)
each (see Note:)
1/2 cup (40 g) star anise,
2 cups (1/2 l) water,
6 ¹/₂ tbsp (100 ml) olive oil,
1 ¹/₂ tsp Ricard,
1 carrot cut into thin strips,
1 leek cut into thin strips,
A few peppercorns,
Salt,
1 clove garlic,
2 small tomatoes (1 green, 1 red) peeled,
seeded, and cut into 8 wedges,
4 wedges of orange (preferably a blood
orange),
1/3 cup (10 g) chopped fresh coriander
(Chinese parsley) leaves,
1 pinch fresh tarragon leaves,
A few peppercorns.

Preparation:
Scale the fish and clean them; keep the liver
from each fish for making the sauce.

Place the star anise and the water in a
saucepan, bring to a boil, then remove from
the heat. Leave the anise to infuse in the
water for 30 minutes or until cool, then add
the olive oil and the Ricard.

Put half of the carrot and leek strips in a large
frying pan (sauteuse), lay the fish on top of
these vegetables, pour the infusion of anise
over the fish, then cover the fish with the
remaining carrot and leek strips as well as
the peppercorns, salt, garlic, tomato and
orange segments. Cook over a high heat until
the liquid boils, then remove the pan from the
heat and cover. Leave the fish to infuse in
the hot liquid for about 10 minutes.

While the fish are cooking, place their livers
in a mortar with the coriander leaves and
pound to a paste. When the fish are cooked,
stir 8 tablespoons of their cooking liquid into
the pounded ingredients to make a sauce.
Lift the fish out of the liquid in which they

were cooked and place three of them on each
plate. Remove the vegetables and orange
segments from the pan and arrange
them around the fish. Sprinkle fresh tarragon
leaves and a few peppercorns over each
serving. Spoon a tablespoonful of the cooking
liquid and 2 tablespoonfuls of the sauce over
each plate and serve.

*Note: The true red mullet is unknown in the
U.S., but a similar fish called the Red
Goatfish or red mullet (surmulet) is found
all along the Atlantic coast - particularly in
the south among the Florida keys and near
Puerto Rico.*

Pigeon Pot au Feu with Star Anise, Fried Ravioli, and Poached Pigeon Eggs.

*Pot-au-feu de pigeons ramiers à l'anis étoilé,
ravioli en chausson, et œufs de pigeon
pochés.*

Ingredients for 4 servings:
5 wood pigeons or squab (1 for bouillon only).

For the marinade:
1 tbsp red wine vinegar,
6 ¹/₂ tbsp (100 ml) olive oil,
1 slice of onion,
Salt, pepper,
1 tbsp Ricard.

For the bouillon:
8 ³/₄ cups (2 l) water,
1 carrot, sliced,
1 small onion, sliced,
1 leek, sliced,
3 branches celery,
2 tbsp (30 g) coarse salt,
1/3 cup (30 g) star anise,
2 tbsp (15 g) peppercorns,
Bouquet garni.

For the vegetable garnish:
8 baby carrots, peeled,
8 tiny leeks, cleaned,
1 heart of celery, cut into quarters,
5 oz (150 g) salsify (oyster plant), peeled and
cut into 2-inch (5 cm) pieces.

For the ravioli:
3 tbsp (50 ml) heavy cream,
A dash of Ricard,
Salt, pepper,
3 ¹/₂ oz (100 g) short pastry dough,
Breadcrumbs,
6 ¹/₂ tbsp (100 g) clarified butter,
4 pigeon eggs,
4 small toasted pieces of bread,
4 slices poached bone marrow.

Preparation:
For the marinade. Remove the hearts, livers
and gizzards from the birds; clean the
gizzards and keep aside with the livers and
hearts. Put one pigeon aside for making the
bouillon.

Take the other four birds, slice off each
breast and wing in one piece, and cut off the
legs (thigh and drumstick). Save the carcass
of each bird for making the bouillon.
Place the livers, hearts, gizzards, legs and
breasts in an earthenware platter, add the
other ingredients for the marinade, and
leave to marinate while making the bouillon.

For the bouillon. Place the water in a large
pot, add the whole pigeon set aside earlier,
the carcasses of the other four birds, the star
anise and peppercorns tied in a cloth and all
the other ingredients for the bouillon. Bring
to a boil and skim off any foam that appears,
then lower the heat and simmer, covered, for
1 hour. Strain and keep the bouillon.

For the vegetable garnish. Cook the
vegetables separately by boiling each one for
5 minutes in salted water, then discard
half of the water in which they were cooked
and replace it with an equal amount of
bouillon. Keep warm.

Making the ravioli and eggs. Take the pigeon
legs from the marinade, bone them and chop
the meat with a sharp knife. Place the meat
in a bowl with the cream, then add the Ricard
and a little salt and pepper. Mix well
and refrigerate while making the dough.

Roll out the dough and cut it into 4 squares;
place a quarter of the chilled filling on each
piece of dough, then fold the dough over to
enclose the filling. Wet the edges of the
dough lightly to make them stick together.
When ready to serve, roll each ravioli

in breadcrumbs and fry them in the clarified
butter until golden brown on both sides:
In the same pan, fry the hearts, livers,
gizzards, and breast meat from the marinade.
Salt and pepper to taste.

Poach the pigeon eggs in a pot with some of
the bouillon.

To serve:
Serve in a large soup bowl. In each bowl,
place one ravioli, arrange the other fried
ingredients, salt and pepper lightly.
Place some of the vegetable garnish in each
bowl, and spoon in enough hot bouillon to fill.
Add a piece of toasted bread topped with
poached bone marrow to each bowl, then
place a poached egg in the center and serve.

Jacques Guy "Le Petit Relais."

Jacques Guy was born on June 7, 1944 in the town of Bourg-en-Bresse. He began his career as an apprentice chef in Nantua at the Hôtel de France. He later moved to the Auberge du Père Bise in Talloires, then became head chef at the Auberge Bressanne in his native Bourg-en-Bresse, where he worked for five years. In 1969 he bought and restored a beautiful 15th century house which has now become his restaurant, Le Petit Relais. Jacques Guy won his first Michelin star in 1977.

Corn Crêpes with Ricard.

Les crêpes de maïs au Ricard.

Ingredients for 12 servings:
cups (800 g) fresh corn kernels,
generous cup (150 g) flour,
tbsp heavy cream,
medium eggs,
1/2 tsp granulated sugar,
tsp Ricard,
Butter (for the crêpe pans).

Preparation:
Cook the corn in boiling salted water and
drain. Place the corn in an electric blender
and blend to make a smooth puree, add
successively the flour, cream, eggs, sugar
and Ricard. Blend until smooth, then pour
the batter into a bowl.

Heat a little butter in very small crêpe pans,
then add a ladleful of batter and cook over
high heat. Brown the crêpes on both sides,
then drain on absorbant paper to remove any
excess fat. Use several small pans and keep
the cooked crêpes warm in the oven while
making the remaining ones. Serve hot.

Brill Fillets with Shallot Butter Sauce.

Le suprême de barbue au beurre d'échalotes.

Ingredients for 4 servings:
1 brill (or other flatfish) weighing 4 lbs
(1.8 kg),
Fish stock,
4 shallots, finely chopped,
6 1/2 tbsp (100 ml) white wine,
1 tbsp vinegar,
6 1/2 tbsp (100 g) butter, softened and broken
into 15 pieces,
1 tbsp heavy cream,
1 tbsp Ricard,
1 pinch saffron.

For the garnish:
4 crayfish "à la nage" or puff pastry
squares,
Spinach and mushrooms sauteed in butter.

Preparation:
Clean and fillet the fish. Place the fillets in a
large frying pan with just enough fish stock
to cover them. Poach over low heat for 6
to 8 minutes, then remove from the heat and
cover while preparing the sauce.

Boil the shallots in the white wine and
vinegar in a saucepan until almost all the
liquid has evaporated, then add the butter,
whisking constantly as if making a *beurre
blanc*. The saucepan should be away from the
heat or in a *bain-marie* when adding the
butter.

Salt and pepper the sauce, whisk in the
cream, one tablespoon of the stock in which
the fish was cooked and the Ricard. Add the
saffron, whisking vigorously.

Lift the fish fillets out of their cooking liquid,
place on dinner plates, spoon the sauce over
them and serve.

The plates may be garnished with crayfish
cooked *à la nage* or squares of puff pastry, as
well as spinach and mushrooms that have
been quickly sauteed in butter.

In the Heart of Landes

Michel Guérard.
Les Prés et les Sources d'Eugénie.
Eugénie-les-Bains, (Landes).

Spiny lobsters cooked in seaweed with
madonna sauce.

Rabbit with glazed turnips and greens.

Robert Garrapit
Hôtel-Restaurant Europe,
Villeneuve-de-Marsan, (Landes).

Asparagus with woodsman's sauce.

Skewered angler-fish and prunes.

Michel Guérard "Les Prés et les Sources d'Eugénie."

Michel Guérard was born in 1933 in Vetheuil. He worked as an apprentice chef for Kleber-Alix in Mantes, where he became first pastry chef, then chef saucier. He then worked several years for a private employer, before returning to restaurant work with Jean Delaveyne at the Camélia de Bougival, near Paris.

In 1965 he opened his own restaurant, a small bistrot, in Asnières (a suburb of Paris). This restaurant, the famous Pot-au-Feu, was for years one of the favorite dining spots of Parisians.

Michel Guérard is one of the most talented chefs of his generation. Since 1972 he has lived and worked in the south-west of France in Eugénie-les-Bains. In the quiet of his country kitchen, he developed his *Cuisine Minceur,* now famous throughout the world. It is here also that he created his *Cuisine Gourmande,* with which he won the highest distinction attributed to any restaurant in France - 3 stars in the Michelin Guide.

Spiny Lobsters Cooked in Seaweed with Madonna Sauce.

Langoustes sous les algues à la sauce vierge.

Ingredients for 6 servings:
For the Madonna Sauce:
3 tomatoes, peeled, seeded and chopped,
1 tsp fresh dill, chopped,
1/2 tsp Ricard,
2 cloves garlic, unpeeled,
2 tbsp chopped parsley,
1 tbsp chopped tarragon,
8 coriander seeds, coarsley crushed,
3/4 cup (200 ml) olive oil,
Salt, pepper.

For the lobsters:
2 large handfuls fresh seaweed (see Note),
3/4 cup (200 ml) cold water,
3 spiny lobsters 1 lb 10 oz (750 g) each.

Preparation:
The Madonna Sauce. Place all the ingredients for the sauce into a saucepan, simmer very slowly over very low heat (or in a double boiler) for 30 minutes. Slow cooking gives the sauce time to ripen and develop its flavor. Serve warm, as described below. This sauce is also excellent with other fish, salads, and cold chicken.

Cooking the lobsters. Cover the bottom of a large pot with a layer of fresh seaweed. add the water, then place the lobsters in the pot and cover them with more seaweed. Cover the pot and cook over very high heat for 20 minutes.

To serve:
When the lobsters are cooked, take the pot to the table, and open it before your guests so that they can smell the freshness of the sea, then return to the kitchen to cut and serve the lobsters. Remove the lobsters from the pot, and split them open lengthwise with a long sharp knife. Place one half lobster on each plate, scoop out the small grainy pouch in the head, spoon the sauce over the lobster, and serve.

Note: Lobster, oysters, and other shellfish are sometimes sold packed in seaweed; ask for it where you buy fish.

Rabbit with Glazed Turnips and Greens.

Baron de lapereau mange-tout.

Ingredients for 2 servings:
For the turnips:
12 baby turnips with their greens,
4 1/3 cups (1 l) water,
2 tsp (15 g) coarse salt,
3 tbsp (45 g) butter,
Salt, pepper,
2 tsp (10 g) sugar.

For the rabbit:
Saddle and legs from a 2 lb 10 oz (1.2 kg) rabbit,
1 1/2 tbsp (20 g) butter,
Salt, pepper,
1 1/2 cups, tightly packed (40 g) fresh spinach (washed, stems removed),
6 1/2 tbsp (100 ml) chicken stock.

For the sauce:
3/4 tsp Ricard,
1 1/2 tbsp (20 g) butter, softened,
Salt, pepper.

Preparation:
Cooking the turnips. Cut off all but 1 1/4 inches (3 cm) of the greens from the young turnips. Place the water and coarse salt in a pot, bring to a boil and add the turnip greens. Boil for just 1 minute, then drain. Set aside for later use.

Peel the turnips with a potato peeler leaving the tuft of greens. Place the turnips in a frying pan (*sauteuse*), add enough water to barely cover them (they should not float), 3 tablespoons (45 g) butter, salt, pepper and the sugar. Cook uncovered at a moderate boil (about 18 minutes) until all of the water has evapored. Then shake the pan so that the turnips will roll in the syrupy mixture of sugar and butter and become shiny. If the turnips are not to be served immediately, leave a little liquid in the pan and then finish reducing the liquid just before serving.

Cooking the rabbit. In an oval pot, heat 1 1/2 tablespoons (20 g) butter and brown the rabbit on all sides. This should take about 4 minutes over medium heat. Salt and pepper the rabbit lightly, then add the spinach and

turnip greens to the pot. Cover the pot and continue cooking over medium heat for 5 minutes.

Lift the rabbit out of the pot. With a large sharp knife, cut the rabbit in half at the end of the back (saddle) and beginning of the legs. Place the saddle of rabbit on a plate and cover with aluminum foil. Keep warm in a 325°F (160°C) oven with the door ajar while the legs finish cooking. Put the legs back into the pot, add the stock, cover and cook for another 5 minutes. Using a slotted spoon, lift out the legs, as well as the spinach and greens, and put them all on the plate in the oven to stay warm while preparing the sauce.

Making the sauce. Boil the remaining liquid in which the rabbit has cooked until it has reduced by about a third, then add the Ricard, and 1 1/2 tablespoonfuls (20 g) butter, a little at a time. Shake the pot as the butter is being added to make the sauce spin around the sides of the pot. Once all the butter has been added, keep the sauce warm, but do not let it boil.

Robert Garrapit "Hôtel-Restaurant Europe".

Robert Garrapit was born on January 9, 1938 in Villeneuve-de-Marsan. His father was a baker but Robert wanted to become a cook. He worked as an apprentice chef in Pau with Mr. Pucheux of the Hôtel du Commerce from 1952 to 1956.

After finishing compulsory military service, Robert and his family bought and opened the Hotel-Restaurant Europe in Villeneuve-de-Marsan. There Robert Garrapit directs the kitchens and prepares authentic local dishes as well as some of his own inventions which reflect his humor, friendliness, and refinement.

Asparagus with Woodsman's Sauce.

La botte d'asperges landaises à la sauce bûcheron.

Ingredients for 4 servings:
3 ¹/₃ lbs (1.5 kg) fresh white asparagus,
Lambs' lettuce (corn salad) or other green salad,
Mousseline sauce,
Fresh herbs (chervil, parsley, chives, tarragon),
A dash of Ricard (to taste),
Pine nuts.

Preparation:
Peel the asparagus, using a vegetable peeler, then tie them into bunches of 4 to 5 asparagus each. Drop the asparagus into a large pot of boiling salted water, and boil for 20 to 25 minutes. Do not let the asparagus boil too rapidly, since this could damage the tips. Drain the asparagus and serve immediately; or leave them in the water they cooked in, away from the heat, keeping them warm until serving.

Lay on a serving platter a bed of fresh lambs' lettuce (or other salad greens); place the asparagus on top, and serve. At the same time, serve a sauce boat of mousseline sauce to which a mixture of freshly chopped chervil, parsley, chives, and tarragon have been added. Add a little Ricard to the sauce, then, in the best Landaise tradition, sprinkle grilled pine nuts over the sauce just before serving.

Skewered Angler-Fish and Prunes.

Les brochettes de lotte Gerland.

Ingredients for 4 servings:
24 stoneless prunes,
4 tbsp armagnac (or cognac),
1 lb 5 oz (600 g) angler-fish, skinned (see Note),
5 oz (150 g) prosciutto (or bacon),
2 cups (1/2 l) crayfish sauce (coulis),
1 tbsp Ricard.

Preparation:
Soak the prunes in a bowl with the armagnac for 2 hours. Cut the fish into small pieces. Skewer a piece of fish, then a prune, then a piece of ham; continue in this manner until 4 skewers have been made with all the ingredients. Season with salt and pepper. Cook on a grill over hot coals or under the broiler.

Serve with a crayfish sauce (*coulis*) to which a little Ricard has been added at the last minute.

Note: The true angler-fish is a European fish; in the U.S. a similar Atlantic fish, called the goosefish, can be used instead. The flesh of the angler-fish is firm, white, and somewhat resembles lobster meat. The meat from lobster tails may be used instead of angler-fish in this recipe.

Travelling Through Alsace.

Jean-Pierre et Paul Haeberlin.
Auberge de l'Ill, Illhaeusern, (Haut-Rhin).

Puff pastry with poached egg and frogs' legs.

Tenderloin fillet roast with cucumbers.

René Fulgraff.
Au Fer Rouge, Colmar, (Haut-Rhin).

Sea bass and salmon with herbs.

Bavarian cream with fruit.

Jean Pierre et Paul Haeberlin "Auberge de l'Ill".

Paul Haeberlin was born on November 24, 1923 in the Alsacian town of Illhaeusern. He remained in his native Alsace working as an apprentice with Weber in Ribeauville from 1939 until 1945. Then, when drafted into the Army, he was chef to Major General de Lattre de Tassigny before setting out for Paris where he worked at the Rôtisserie Périgourdine and at the Poccardy until 1950.

Returning to Alsace, Paul and his brother Jean-Pierre took charge of the family's restaurant. The Auberge de l'Ill is beautifully located on the banks of a stream, and surrounded by a magnificent garden. Paul Haeberlin has become the region's leading chef, he and his brother serve guests from all over France in their now famous restaurant.

Paul works in the kitchen preparing brilliant dishes from a wide selection of the best local products; Jean-Pierre welcomes customers with charming hospitality. The Haeberlin brothers were awarded their third Michelin star in 1967.

Puff Pastry with Poached Egg and Frogs' Legs.

Le feuilleté d'œuf poché aux cuisses de grenouilles.

Ingredients for 4 servings:
9 oz (250 g) puff pastry dough,
6 ¹/₂ tbsp (100 g) butter,
2 shallots, finely chopped,
24 pairs of frogs' legs,
1 cup (125 ml) dry white wine (preferably Riesling),
1 cup (125 ml) fish stock,
1/2 clove garlic, finely chopped,
1 tsp Ricard,
Salt, pepper,
2 tsp soft butter mixed with 2 tsp flour,
3 tbsp heavy cream,
Juice of 1/2 lemon,
1 generous tsp chopped parsley,
1 generous tsp chopped chives,
4 eggs.

Preparation:
Making the pastry. Preheat the oven to 400°F (200°C). Roll the puff pastry dough into a square approximately 8 inches (20 cm) on a side, then cut into four smaller squares. Place the squares of pastry on a baking sheet and set aside for 30 minutes, then bake in the preheated oven for 15 to 18 minutes or until golden brown.

Making the garnish. While the dough is sitting, melt half of the butter in a saucepan, then add the shallots and brown lightly. Add the frogs' legs, the white wine, fish stock, garlic and Ricard. Salt and pepper, bring barely to a boil, then lower the heat and simmer uncovered for 10 minutes.

Lift the frogs' legs out of the pot with a slotted spoon, bone them, then set aside on a plate.

Boil the frogs' legs cooking liquid rapidly uncovered, until reduced by half, then lower the heat to a gentle boil. Stir in the butter-flour mixture, then add the cream and lemon juice. Whisk or swirl in the remaining butter, a few pieces at a time; do not allow the sauce to boil. When all the butter has been added, add the meat from the frogs' legs, the chopped parsley and chives. Keep warm.

While the puff pastry is baking, fill a saucepan with water, add the vinegar, and bring barely to a boil. Do not salt the water. Break the eggs into the water, one by one, folding the white over the yolk. Poach the eggs for 4 minutes, then lift them out of the saucepan with a slotted spoon and place them in a basin of cold water.

To serve:
When the pastry has finished baking, remove from the oven and raise the temperature to 450°F (235°C). Cut the pastry down the middle, forming two halves, top and bottom. Place a poached egg (it should still be slightly warm) on the bottom half of each pastry, spoon the sauce over the eggs, then cover with the top of the pastry. Place in the oven for 30 seconds, then serve.

Note: This dish can be served as a main dish for 2 people. Roll the pastry dough into 2 squares. When cooked, garnish each square with pureed spinach and 2 poached eggs in addition to the frogs' legs sauce (see photo).

Tenderloin Fillet Roast with Cucumbers.

Filet de bœuf aux concombres.

Ingredients for 4 servings:
For the beef:
1 ³/₄ lb (800 g) tenderloin filet of beef, for roasting,
3 ¹/₂ oz (100 g) pork fatback (fresh fatty bacon),
2 tbsp (30 g) soft butter,
2 tbsp cooking oil.

For the vegetables:
1 medium (250 g) cucumber,
1 tbsp (15 g) butter (for cucumber),
1/4 large sweet red pepper,
2 tsp butter (for pepper).

For the sauce:
3 shallots, finely chopped,
3/4 cup (200 ml) veal stock,
2 tsp Ricard,
2 tbsp heavy cream,
3 tbsp (45 g) butter,
Salt, pepper.

Preparation:
Preheat the oven to 475°F (245°C). Cut the fatback into long thin strips and lard the tenderloin, or have the butcher do this for you. When larded, rub the beef with 2 tablespoons (30 g) butter and the cooking oil. Place in the oven and roast for 20 minutes, then remove from the oven. Keep the roast warm, but allow to sit for 10 minutes, so that it will be evenly pink all the way through.

Peel the cucumber and cut it into matchstick sized slivers. Parboil for 1 minute, then drain. Melt 1 tablespoon (15 g) butter in a frying pan and sauté the cucumber until tender and beginning to brown. Dice the sweet red pepper and sauté in 2 teaspoons (10 g) butter.

Remove the roast from the roasting pan, place on a platter, and put back in the warm oven while you prepare the sauce.

On top of the stove, brown the shallots in the roasting pan, then deglaze with the veal stock and Ricard. Stir all the pan juices into the liquid, bring to a boil, and allow to reduce by a third. Add the cream, then remove from the heat and add 3 tablespoons (45 g) butter, a few pieces at a time, whisking the sauce vigorously. Taste for seasoning and add salt and pepper if necessary. Add the cucumber and red pepper to the sauce, pour over the roast beef, and serve.

Note: Instead of slicing a large cucumber, 1/2 lb (250 g) fresh gherkins (baby cucumbers) may be used whole, as shown in the photo.

René Fulgraff "Au Fer Rouge."

René Fulgraff was born on October 23, 1954 in Colmar. In 1970 he became an apprentice chef at Pic's in Valence, where he worked for three years. From 1974 to 1975 he worked under Claude Peyrot at the Vivarois restaurant in Paris, and in 1976 with Paul Bocuse.

At the end of 1976, he returned to his family's restaurant where he now directs the kitchens.

Sea Bass and Salmon with Herbs.

Bar et saumon aux herbes.

Ingredients for 6 servings:
1 cup (250 ml) fish stock,
3/4 cup (200 ml) dry white wine,
1/3 cup (80 g) Ricard,
2 tsp herbes de Provence,
3/4 cup (200 ml) heavy cream,
1 1/4 cups (300 g) soft butter,
1/2 lemon,
1 large bulb fennel, cut into "julienne" strips,
3 1/2 tbsp (50 g) butter,
1 lb (500 g) fresh salmon fillets,
1 lb (500 g) fresh sea bass fillets,
Salt, pepper,
Pilaf rice (for garnish).

Preparation:
Making the sauce and cooking the fennel.
Place the fish stock, white wine, Ricard and herbs in a *sauteuse* or saucepan and bring to a boil over high heat. Boil uncovered until the mixture has almost evaporated. It should be very thick and syrupy. Add the cream, bring to a boil, then lower the heat and add the butter little by little, either by whisking it in or swirling it in. Taste for seasoning, add a little more Ricard, salt and pepper if needed, and a squeeze of lemon juice. The sauce should be creamy but not thick; if too thick, add a little fish stock.

Cook the strips of fennel with a little water and 3 1/2 tablespoons (50 g) of butter.

To cook the fish and serve:
Preheat the oven to 475°F (245°C). Thinly slice the salmon and bass fillet, cutting almost horizontal to the table. There should be 6 slices cut from each fish. Lay the slices in a shallow, non-stick roasting pan and place in the oven for 5 to 8 minutes or until cooked.

Cover the bottom of a serving platter with the fennel. Lay alternating slices of salmon and bass on top, then pour the sauce around (not over) the fish. Serve with a dish of Pilaf rice on the side.

Bavarian Cream with Fruit.

Bavarois aux fruits.

Ingredients for 6 servings:
1 cup (250 ml) milk,
1/3 cup (80 g) granulated sugar,
3 egg yolks,
2 tsp (3 sheets) gelatin,
2 tbsp water (if using powdered gelatin),
1 cup (250 ml) heavy cream,
4 tsp (20 ml) Ricard,
2 bananas,
3 kiwi fruits (chinese gooseberries),
2 oranges,
1/2 lb (250 g) strawberries, stems removed.

Preparation:
Making the Bavarian cream. In a saucepan, bring the milk to a boil with half the sugar. Beat the remaining sugar with the egg yolks until the mixture whitens and forms a ribbon, then add the hot milk, beating vigorously with a wire whisk. Pour back into the sauce pan and place over very low heat, stirring constantly with a wooden spoon until the mixture thickens and lightly coats the spoon (do not allow to boil). Remove from the heat.

Moisten the gelatin with the water (if using sheet gelatin, soften it in a large bowl of cold water, then drain) and stir into the hot custard. Allow the mixture to cool completely, stirring occasionally to prevent lumps from forming.

Whip the cream until stiff. When the custard is completely cold and the consistency of very thick cream, fold the whipped cream into it, then gently stir in the Ricard.

To mold and serve:
Peel and slice the bananas and kiwi fruits. Peel the oranges and separate the sections. Wash and drain the strawberries.

Line the bottom of an 8-inch (20 cm) soufflé mold with the kiwi slices, then pour over them 1/4 of the cold Bavarian cream. Place in the refrigerator until set. Cover this layer of cream with the sliced bananas, then pour in another quarter of the cream. Refrigerate until set, then continue layering in the same way with the orange sections, strawberries, and remaining bavarian cream. Chill the finished dessert for at least 2 hours, then turn out and serve.

Note: A little extra fruit may be sliced and used to decorate the dessert once it has been turned out (see photo).

In Paris on the "Rive Gauche"

Alain Senderens.
L'Archestrate, Paris 7e.

Scallops with fennel and Ricard.

Chicken fricassee with Ricard.

Jacques Yvonnou.
Les Glénan, Paris 7e.

Mussels in cream sauce with Ricard.

Fish fillets with Ricard.

Alain Senderens "L'Archestrate."

Alain Senderens was born on December 2, 1939 in Hyères, on the Mediterranean coast. Early in life he decided to become a cook, and at 18 he was apprenticed at a restaurant in the town of Lourdes. He later moved on and eventually came to Paris where he continued his apprenticeship at the Tour d'Argent and at Lucas Carton's, before becoming an assistant chef at the Paris Hilton.

A man who truly loves his profession and full of ideas, Alain Senderens is constantly experimenting with new dishes. He opened a restaurant of his own, a great success, first at its original address on the Rue de l'Exposition, and now at its current address on the Rue de Varenne. His restaurant, L'Archestrate, is filled every day with gourmets who appreciate his inventive and tasty dishes. Those who have dined in his restaurant were not surprised when it was awarded its third star by the Michelin Guide in the spring of 1978.

Scallops with Fennel and Ricard.

Coquilles Saint-Jacques au fenouil et au Ricard.

Ingredients for 4 servings:
16 scallops,
Salt, pepper,
A pinch dried dill, per person,
3/4 tsp Ricard, per person,
1 bulb fennel,
1 tsp butter,
6 1/2 tbsp (100 ml) water,
6 1/2 tbsp (100 g) soft butter, broken into 10 pieces,
3 star anise, per person.

Preparation:
Take the scallops from their shells and wash them under cold water to remove any sand. Place 4 scallops, each on a separate piece of aluminium foil, season with salt, pepper, dill and Ricard. Fold the foil so that all these ingredients are enclosed inside it, making what is called a *papillote*.

Cut the fennel into very fine *julienne* strips and place in a frying pan with butter, water, salt and pepper. Sauté over moderate heat until the fennel softens, then cover and keep warm.

Place the papillotes in a steamer, and steam for 3 minutes, then remove and open the aluminium foil. Pour the juices from the papillotes into a saucepan and boil rapidly until reduced by half. Using a wire whisk, add the butter a little at a time, beating constantly. The sauce should not boil as the butter is being added. Salt and pepper to taste.

To serve:
Spoon the sauce into hot dinner plates, place the scallops in the middle with the cooked fennel around the edge. Garnish each plate with a few star anise, and serve immediately.

Chicken Fricassee with Ricard.

Fricassée de poulet au Ricard.

Ingredients for 4 servings:
1 chicken weighing approx. 3 1/2 lbs (1.6 kg),
Salt, pepper,
4 tbsp (60 g) butter,
1 tbsp olive oil,
1 bulb fennel, chopped,
1 onion, chopped,
2 tsp mild curry powder,
5 tbsp Ricard,
2 tbsp white wine,
2 cups (1/2 l) heavy cream,
1 star anise,
1 tbsp butter, softened,
Salt, pepper,
4 star anise, to garnish.

Preparation:
Cut the chicken into eight pieces and season with salt and pepper. Heat half the butter and the olive oil in a frying pan, add the chicken, and brown over moderate heat for several minutes.

In a second frying pan or *sauteuse,* heat the remaining 2 tablespoons of butter, add the fennel, onion, and curry powder. Stir and cook over low heat for about 5 minutes.

Use two forks or a slotted spoon to lift the pieces of chicken out of their frying pan and place them in the pan with the onion and fennel.

Add the Ricard and white wine to the pan with the fennel, and stir to deglaze the pan. Cover and simmer slowly for a total of 20 minutes. Halfway through the cooking time, a little more Ricard or white wine can be added if the liquid has evaporated too quickly. Once they are cooked, remove the pieces of chicken from the pan with a slotted spoon, cover, and keep warm in the oven.

Use a large spoon to remove as much fat from the pan as possible. Do not remove any of the vegetables. Add the cream and star anise to the pan, and simmer uncovered over very low heat until the sauce begins to thicken. While simmering the sauce, stir it occasionally with a wire whisk. Once the sauce begins to thicken, add a tablespoon of butter and pour the sauce through a strainer. Taste and add salt and pepper if needed.

To serve:
Place the pieces of chicken on a serving platter, spoon the strained sauce over them and garnish with 4 whole star anise. Serve immediately. The chicken can also be served in the pan in which the sauce was cooked.

Jacques Yvonnou "Les Glenan".

Jacques Yvonnou is from Brittany; he was born in Concarneau in 1940. After studying at the Ecole Hôtelière in Paris, he worked for two years in the kitchens at Prunier before becoming maître d'hôtel at Lasserre where he worked for 4 years.

His experience, both in the kitchens and in the dining room, led him to open his own restaurant in 1973 called Les Glénan, where he specializes in preparing seafood fresh from his native Brittany.

Mussels in Cream Sauce with Ricard.

Poêlon de moules au Ricard.

Ingredients for 4 servings:
1 tbsp butter,
1 onion, chopped,
1 bulb fennel, chopped,
2 tbsp Ricard,
3 ½ lbs (2 l) mussels,
1 egg yolk,
6 ½ tbsp (100 ml) double cream,
A pinch chopped tarragon,
Salt, pepper,
Juice of 1 lemon,
Chopped parsley,
Chopped chives.

Preparation:
Heat the butter in a large saucepan, add the onion and fennel, and brown over moderate heat. Add the Ricard and the mussels, cover and cook until the mussels have opened. Pour the mussels into a large strainer over a bowl to retrieve the cooking liquid. Place the liquid in a saucepan and boil to reduce by two-thirds. Remove one shell from each mussel, then place the mussels in an earthenware dish for serving. Once their cooking liquid has been reduced, remove it from the heat and mix with the egg yolks and cream. Sprinkle in the tarragon, salt and pepper to taste, and add the lemon juice. Do not allow to boil. Pour the sauce over the mussels, sprinkle with chopped parsley and chives, and serve immediately.

Fish Fillets with Ricard.

Suprême de daurade au Ricard.

Ingredients for 4 servings:
1 porgy or similar fish weighing 3 lbs 5 oz (1.5 kg), or 4 smaller fish (One per person see Note),
1 carrot, sliced,
1 small onion, sliced,
Small bouquet garni,
2 tbsp Ricard,
Butter,
3 shallots, finely chopped,
6 ½ tbsp (100 ml) white wine,
4 tbsp double cream,
1 ½ tbsp (20 g) soft butter,
Salt, pepper,
Freshly chopped chervil.

Preparation:
Clean and scale the fish, then fillet them with a very sharp knife. Place the bones and head in a saucepan, barely cover with cold water, add the carrot, onion, *bouquet garni* and Ricard to make a fish stock. Boil for 30 minutes, then strain.

Preheat the oven to 475°F (245°C). Butter a roasting pan, add the shallots and white wine, and simmer on top of the stove to soften the shallots. Place the fish fillet in the roasting pan, add the fish stock, and bake in the oven for 15 minutes.

Remove the fillet with a slotted spoon, place on a serving platter and keep warm. Place the roasting pan over high heat and reduce the cooking liquid by two-thirds. Once reduced, stir in the cream and butter, add salt and pepper, then pour the sauce over the fish fillets, sprinkle with chopped chervil, and serve immediately.

Note: Porgy, snapper, sea bream, or almost any other fish can be filleted and cooked in this manner.

Approaching the Auvergne

Pierre et Jean Troisgros.
Hôtel des Frères Troigros, Roanne, (Loire).

Guinea hen steacks "Ricardo".

Banana fritters "Back from China".

Jean-Luc Rostaing.
Le Favières, Saint-Cyr-de-Favières, (Loire).

Castellet shellfish salad.

Snail vol-au-vent à la provençale.

Jean Troisgros was born in 1926, his brother Pierre in 1928, in Chalon-sur-Saône.

Their father, Jean-Baptiste Troisgros ran a cafe in his native Burgundy and encouraged his two sons to become chefs (a profession he had wished to pursue himself). In 1930 he opened a hotel in the town of Roanne which became famous when his sons took over the kitchens.

The two brothers spent several years of apprenticeship learning classic French cuisine at Lucas Carton's in Paris. They later became interested in creative cuisine, when working with Fernand Point at his restaurant in Vienne.

Jean and Pierre Troisgros took over the kitchens in the family restaurant in 1953. They won their first Michelin star in 1955, a second star followed in 1965, and finally they received the coveted third star in 1968. With every passing year their reputation grows in France and throughout the world.

Guinea Hen Steaks "Ricardo".

Aiguillettes de pintade "Ricardo".

Ingredients for 4 servings:
For the marinade:
2 guinea hens weighing 2 lbs 7 oz (1.1 kg) each,
2 ¹/₂ tbsp (40 ml) Ricard,
Salt, pepper,
A pinch thyme.

For the serpentines:
3 carrots,
3 turnips (long),
1 large cucumber.

For the vegetable cake:
3 carrots, cut into thick matchsticks,
3 turnips, cut into thick matchsticks,
2 tsp (10 g) butter,
1 onion, chopped,
3 bulbs fennel,
3 tbsp (50 ml) water,
Salt, pepper.

For the sauce:
2 ¹/₂ tbsp (40 ml) white wine,
2 tbsp (30 g) butter, softened,
Salt, pepper.

Preparation:
Marinating the guinea hens. Cut the legs from the birds. (Keep for use in another recipe.) Carefully cut each breast off the bone in one piece. With a sharp knife, slice each breast lengthwise into three thin *steaks,* thus making a total of 12 steaks from the 4 breasts. Place the steaks on a cutting board between two pieces of oiled parchment paper, and flatten them gently with the flat side of a cleaver. Place the steaks in an earthenware platter with the Ricard, salt, pepper, and a pinch of thyme; marinate for 1 hour.

Making the serpentines. Boil the carrots for 2 minutes then drain. Cut each carrot into pieces about 2 ¹/₂ inches (6 cm) long. With a sharp knife or vegetable peeler, slice off ribbons of carrot as long as possible, cutting as if removing the peel from an orange in one long spiraling band. Turn and slice the carrot

until there is nothing left but the central core, which is discarded. Peel and cut the turnips and cucumber into 2 ¹/₂ inch (6 cm) pieces, then cut them like the carrots into long ribbons or bands. Once all the vegetable ribbons have been prepared, drop them into a pot of rapidly boiling water, then drain and allow to cool.

Make the serpentines by placing a strip of carrot on a strip of cucumber, and covering with a strip of turnip to make three layers all the same length, approximately 8 inches (20 cm). Roll up the vegetables on themselves and tie each roll or serpentine with a little string so that it will hold its shape. Roll all the vegetable ribbons into serpentines.

Making the vegetable cake. In a large pot of boiling salted water, cook the carrot sticks for 8 minutes, remove, then cook the turnips 8 minutes and remove; finally cook the vegetable serpentines 8 minutes and drain. Remove the string from the serpentines. Keep all the vegetables warm until ready to serve. Melt 2 teaspoons (10 g) of butter in a large frying pan, add the onions and brown. Add the fennel, water, salt and pepper. Cover the pot and simmer for 30 minutes.

Generously butter a 8-inch (20 cm) cake pan that is 2 ¹/₂ inches (6 cm) deep. Place the carrot and turnip sticks upright all around the sides of the pan. Fill the pan with fennel, packing it down tightly with a spoon. Place the pan in a large roasting pan, fill the roasting pan with enough boiling water to come half way up the side of the cake pan, and bake in a 400°F (200°C) oven for 20 minutes.

To finish and serve:
Heat a little butter in a large frying pan. Lift the steaks out of their marinade, pat dry in a cloth, and sauté them quickly to color both sides (this should take no more than 2 minutes). If not serving immediately, keep warm after sautéing.

Pour the Ricard from the marinade into the frying pan, add the white wine, stir, and boil until reduced by half, then whisk 2 tablespoons (30 g) butter into the juices in the pan (away from the heat) to make a sauce. Salt and pepper to taste.

Turn the vegetable cake out onto the center of a large serving platter, place the serpentines on top, and the guinea hen steaks all around it. Spoon the sauce over the meat and serve immediately.

Banana Fritters "Back from China".

Beignets de bananes "Retour de Chine".

Ingredients for 4 servings:
For the batter:
3/4 cup (100 g) flour,
5 tsp (25 g) granulated sugar,
1 egg,
A pinch salt,
1 ¹/₃ cups (300 ml) milk.

For the fritters:
4 ripe bananas,
2 tbsp (30 ml) Ricard,
Flour, to coat bananas,
1/2 cup (100 g) sugar,
6 ¹/₂ tbsp (100 ml) water.

To serve:
4 bowls ice water,
Ice cubes,
1 tsp Ricard per bowl.

Preparation:
Making the batter. Place the flour, sugar, egg, salt and milk in a bowl. Stir the milk into the flour with a wooden spoon until the mixture is smooth. Work the batter as little as possible.

Making the fritters. Peel the bananas and cut each one into 8 slices. Leave them to marinate for 10 minutes in 2 ¹/₂ tablespoons (3 ml) of Ricard mixed with a tablespoon of sugar.

Heat the oil in a deep frier until very hot, 300°F (150°C). Remove the bananas from the marinade, roll them in flour to coat them lightly, then dip them in the batter and deep fry for about 2 minutes. Lift the fritters out of the frier and drain on absorbent paper.

Place 1/2 cup (100 g) sugar and 6 ¹/₂ tablespoons (100 ml) water in a saucepan and cook until a light caramel is formed.

Use a fork to dip each fritter into the caramel, coat completely, then lift out of the caramel. Place the caramelized fritters on an oiled baking sheet (keep them from touching) and keep warm.

To serve:
Place a bowl containing several ice cubes, ice water, and a teaspoon of Ricard before each guest. Place the hot fritters on 4 plates. Serve a plate of fritters to each guest, who should scrape the fritters into the ice water to harden the caramel, and immediately lift them out with a fork and eat them.

Note: Some of the bananas can be cut in half lengthwise, rather than in circles, as shown in the photo.

Jean-Luc Rostaing "Le Favières."

Jean-Luc Rostaing was born November 8, 1948 in the town of Vienne. He started work as an apprentice in the restaurant La Poularde in Montrond-les-Bains from 1963 to 1965. The following year he moved to the Bas-Bréau restaurant in Barbizon. From 1966 to 1967 he studied with Paul Bocuse in Collonges, and from 1967 to 1968 with Paul Blanc at the Chapon Fin in Thoissey. He then spent a year in the Army as cook at the Amirauté de Papeete in Tahiti. Since 1973 he has been the chef in Le Favières his family's restaurant.

Snail Vol-au-Vent à la Provençale.

Feuilleté d'escargots à la provençale.

Ingredients for 4 servings:
For the snails:
48 live snails,
4 ¹/₃ cups (1 l) white wine,
8 ³/₄ cups (2 l) water,
Salt, pepper,
Bouquet garni,
2 cloves garlic, unpeeled,
2 cloves,
3 coriander seeds,
1 star anise.

For the sauce:
2 cups (1/2 l) heavy cream,
3 tomatoes, peeled, seeded and finely chopped,
Parsley, finely chopped,
2 cloves garlic, finely chopped,
6 ¹/₂ tbsp (100 g) butter, softened and broken into 10 pieces,
2 tbsp (30 ml) Ricard,

4 vol-au-vent pastry shells, 4 in (10 cm) in diameter, baked just before filling.

Preparation:
If using live snails, place them in a closed container with an opening for air and leave to fast for 2 to 3 days. Wash the snails in cold water to which a handful of coarse salt has been added.

Break open each snail shell and take out the snail, then discard the shells. Place the snails in a large pot with the white wine, water, salt, pepper, *bouquet garni,* garlic, cloves, coriander, and star anise. Bring to a boil, then lower the heat and simmer slowly for 3 hours. Remove the snails from the cooking liquid and boil the liquid until it has reduced by two-thirds. In another saucepan, boil the cream until it has been reduced by half. Pour the reduced cooking liquid through a strainer, place in a saucepan, and add the reduced cream, tomatoes, parsley, and garlic. Boil the sauce, remove from the heat and whisk or swirl in the butter, and finally the Ricard. Add the snails to the finished sauce and use this mixture to fill the pastry shells just before serving. Serve very hot.

Castellet Shellfish Salad.

Salade de crustacés Castellet.

Ingredients for 6 servings:
For the mayonnaise:
1 egg yolk,
Peanut oil,
4 tsp (20 ml) Ricard,
2 large truffles, 1 ¹/₂ oz (40 g) each, cut into thin julienne strips,
24 boiled crayfish tails, shelled and sliced in half lengthwise,
12 boiled langoustine or large shrimp tails, sliced in half lengthwise,
A 1 lb (500 g) boiled lobster.

To serve:
1 lettuce,
3 tomatoes,
Fresh chervil,
15 boiled crayfish (optional).

For the fennel salad:
1 bulb fennel, thinly sliced,
Meat from 2 large crabs, in pieces,
Olive oil,
Juice of 1 lemon.

Preparation:
Remove the meat from the tail and claws of the lobster. Cut the tail meat into thin slices. Make a mayonnaise using the egg yolk and peanut oil, or any other oil without a strong flavor. Once made, add the Riccard to the mayonnaise with the truffles, langoustines or shrimp, crayfish and lobster tails.

Mix the fennel in a bowl with the meat from the lobster claws broken into small pieces, and the crab meat. Stir in a little olive oil and lemon juice, to taste.

To serve:
Arrange the lettuce leaves on a serving platter, place the fennel salad in the center, and pour the mayonnaise mixture over it. Sprinkle with freshly chopped chervil, place tomato slices all around the edge of the platter and serve.

The salad may also be mixed in a similar manner in a large bowl and decorated with boiled crayfish as shown in the photo opposite.

In Sunny Provence

Roger Vergé.
Le Moulin de Mougins, Mougins,
(Alpes-Maritimes).

Chilled melon balls with fresh tarragon
leaves.

Mint and Ricard parfait.

Alain Carro.
Auberge du Puits Jaubert, Saint-Cassien,
(Var).

Sea bass fillet with sea urchins and cream
sauce.

Veal steaks à la Marseillaise.

Roger Vergé "Le Moulin de Mougins."

Roger Vergé was born in Commentry in 1930. His father was a blacksmith from the Auvergne, his mother came from the Bourbonnais region. After working as an apprentice cook and pastry chef in his home town, Roger Vergé went on a travelling apprenticeship in the best restaurants of France, Switzerland, and Algeria. His preference for sunny climates lured him to Africa, where he managed restaurants for an airline company from 1956 to 1960. In 1961 he returned to France as head chef at Le Club in Cavalière on the Côte d'Azur. There he won a reputation as a fine cook and two Michelin stars.

In 1969 he opened his own restaurant, near Cannes. Thanks to the quality of the light and inventive cuisine developed by Vergé, the Moulin de Mougins has now become the most famous restaurant on the Mediterranean coast.

In 1974 Roger Vergé was awarded his third star by the Michelin Guide.

Chilled Melon Balls with Fresh Tarragon Leaves.

Petits melons charentais rafraîchis aux tendres feuilles d'estragon.

Ingredients for 2 servings:
*2 muskmelons, or cantaloupes, weighing
14 oz (400 g) each,
2 tbsp granulated sugar,
3 tbsp Ricard,
20 fresh tarragon leaves.*

Preparation:
Using a knife, cut each melon in half. With a spoon scoop out the seeds from each melon, and with a melon ball cutter scoop out as many melon balls as possible.

Place the melon balls in a bowl. Scoop out whatever pulp remains in each melon with a spoon, place this in an electric blender (or foodmill) with the sugar and Ricard. Blend to make a smooth purée, then pour this over the melon balls. Add the tarragon leaves to the bowl and stir gently to mix all the ingredients. Fill a serving dish with this mixture and refrigerate for 2 hours before serving.

Mint and Ricard Parfait.

Parfait glacé au Ricard.

Ingredients for 6 servings:
*1/2 cup (125 g) granulated sugar,
5 to 6 tbsp water,
6 egg yolks,
2 tbsp (30 g) granulated sugar,
2/3 cup (150 ml) milk,
3 tbsp (50 ml) mint concentrate or syrup,
3 egg yolks,
3/4 cup (200 ml) heavy cream, refrigerated for whipping,
5 tsp (25 g) granulated sugar,
3 tbsp Ricard.*

Preparation:
Place 1/2 cup (125 g) of sugar in a saucepan with the water, bring to a boil and stir to dissolve the sugar. Remove the pan from the heat and pour the warm syrup into a double boiler containing 6 egg yolks. Stir constantly as the syrup is being added. Beat the warm mixture with a wire whisk until it begins to thicken and foam (about 7 or 8 minutes).

Remove the upper part of the double boiler and continue whisking the mixture until it has completely cooled. Put aside while making the mint ice cream.

Boil 2 tablespoons (30 g) of sugar with the milk. When the sugar has dissolved, pour the mixture into a bowl containing 3 egg yolks, whisking constantly. Allow the mixture to cool completely, then add the mint concentrate and freeze in an electric ice cream freezer. Once the ice cream is made, pour it into a 6 2/3 cup (1 1/2 l) ice cream mold so that it will coat the sides of the mould with a layer of ice cream no more than 3/4 inch (2 cm) thick. Place in the freezer while finishing the cream filling. If there is any mint ice cream left over after coating the mould, use it, melted, as a sauce when serving the parfait.

Beat the cream with a wire whisk until it starts to stiffen, then add 5 teaspoons (25 g) of sugar and continue beating until quite stiff. Whisk the syrup-egg mixture prepared earlier for 2 or 3 minutes until it is about the same temperature as the cream, then beat the Ricard into this mixture. With a slotted spoon, fold this into the whipped cream until the two elements are perfectly homogenous.

Pour this mixture into the ice cream mould to fill it, then place the mould in the freezer for at least 6 hours before serving. When ready to serve, dip the mold into hot water and turn out onto a serving platter.

Alain Carro "Auberge du Puits Jaubert."

Alain Carro was born March 7, 1953 in Saint-Raphaël. After studying at the École Hôtelière in Nice, he worked for two years with Roger Vergé at the Moulin de Mougins. He then spent a year with Michel Guérard in Eugénie-les-Bains before moving to Alsace to work with the Haeberlin brothers in Illhaeusern.

Since January 1978, he has owned and run his own restaurant, the Auberge du Puits Jaubert, situated in the beautiful and restful countryside of Saint-Cassien, inland from the busy Côte d'Azur.

Sea Bass Fillet with Sea Urchins and Cream Sauce.

Suprême de loup au corail d'oursins.

Ingredients for 2 servings:
For the fillets:
3 ¹/₂ tbsp (50 g) butter,
1 sea bass weighing approx. 1 lb 5 oz (600 g),
fileted and skinned, each fillet cut into
4 pieces, approx. 2 oz (50 g) each,
1 lb (500 g) fresh spinach, cleaned, parboiled
for 2 minutes, and drained.

For the tomatoes:
1 tbsp (10 g) garlic, finely chopped,
3 tbsp (50 ml) Ricard,
2 medium (300 g) tomatoes, peeled, seeded
and finely chopped,
1 pinch fresh tarragon,
Salt, pepper.

For the onion rings:
1/2 medium (50 g) onion, sliced into rings,
3/4 cup (200 ml) milk,
Flour,
2 cups (1/2 l) cooking oil.

For the sauce:
1 cup (250 ml) fish stock,
3/4 cup (200 ml) heavy cream,
Orange "tongues" (coral) from 12 sea
urchins (for garnish).

Preparation:
Heat the butter in a frying pan until it begins to brown. Salt and pepper the fish fillets, and fry them in the hot butter for 4 minutes on a side. Lift the fish out of the pan with a spatula and place each fillet on a spinach leaf. Roll up the fillets in the spinach and keep them warm while making the sauce and garnish.

Pour the butter out of the pan the fish was cooked in, then add the garlic and cook over moderate heat until it softens. Add the Ricard to the pan, stirring constantly, then add the tomatoes, tarragon, salt and pepper. Simmer for 12 minutes.

While the tomatoes are cooking, dip each onion ring into the milk, then into the flour

and deep fry them in very hot cooking oil for approximately 10 minutes and drain. Keep them warm.

Boil the fish stock rapidly until reduced by half, then add the cream and continue boiling until the sauce is thick enough to coat a spoon.

To serve:
Spoon the sauce over the dinner plates or onto one large serving platter. Arrange the fish fillets in spinach in a circle around the dish. Place the tomatoes in the center of the dish, top with the onion rings, garnish with the meat from the sea urchins, and serve immediately.

Veal Steaks à la Marseillaise.

Grenadin de veau à la Marseillaise.

Ingredients for 4 servings:
2 tbsp (20 g) shelled pistacios,
1 lb (500 g) salsify (oyster plant), peeled and
cut into 2-inch (5 cm) pieces,
2 ¹/₂ tbsp (40 g) butter, for the salsify,
Chopped parsley, to garnish,
2 ¹/₂ tbsp (40 g) butter, for the veal,
4 veal steaks from the loin or leg, weighing
approx. 5 oz (150 g) each,
Salt, pepper,
Flour,
3 tbsp (50 ml) Ricard,
2/3 cup (150 ml) chicken stock,
6 ¹/₂ tbsp (100 ml) double cream,
Pinch powdered saffron.

Preparation:
Remove the skin from the pistacios by dropping them into boiling water and then removing them from the heat; the skin will come off easily.

Cook the salsify for 15 minutes in boiling salted water, then drain and cool under cold running water. Heat 2 ¹/₂ tablespoons (40 g) of butter in a frying pan, sauté the salsify to reheat, and sprinkle with chopped parsley just before serving.

Heat 2 ¹/₂ tablespoons (40 g) butter in a

second frying pan. Salt and pepper the veal and flour lightly. Cook over moderate heat for about 8 minutes on a side. Lift out the meat and keep it warm while making the sauce.

Pour the butter out of the pan, deglaze with the Ricard and stock, then boil and reduce the liquid for about 5 minutes. Add the cream and continue reducing until the sauce coats a spoon. Add a pinch of saffron to the sauce for color just before serving.

To serve:
Serve in the pan in which the meat was cooked. Place the veal back into the pan surrounded by the salsify. Top each piece of meat with pistacios, and serve immediately.

Note: Veal cutlets may be used instead of loin steaks in this recipe. For those who prefer a more substantial vegetable, use twice as much salsify. The ingredients for the sauce may be doubled for a more copious serving.

Ricard Cocktails

Ricard makes a very refreshing drink when mixed à la Française with 5 parts ice water to 1 part Ricard.

It is equally pleasing as a base for cocktails, as it mixes well with various spirits and fruit juices from all over the world.

It is for this reason that the best international bar-tenders, and the great French chefs have been using Ricard for years in many of their creations.

Ricard Parrot
(Irish Style)

1 oz Ricard,
A few drops of peppermint,
5 oz of iced water (or lemonade).

Ricard Fruit Juice
(German Style)

1 oz Ricard,
5 oz orange juice
(grapefruit or pine apple), ice.

Ricard à la Française
(French Style)

1 measure of Ricard,
5 measures of ice water.

Café Ricard
(Canadian Style)

3/4 oz Ricard,
4 oz hot black coffee,
1/4 oz Triple Sec,
1 tablespoonful of whipped cream.

Pink Ricard
(American Style)

1 oz Ricard,
A few drops of grenadine,
5 oz of lemonade (or iced water).

Ricard Bitter Lemon
(British Style)

1 oz Ricard,
3 oz bitter lemon (lemonade or tonic).

Salambo instead of grenadine

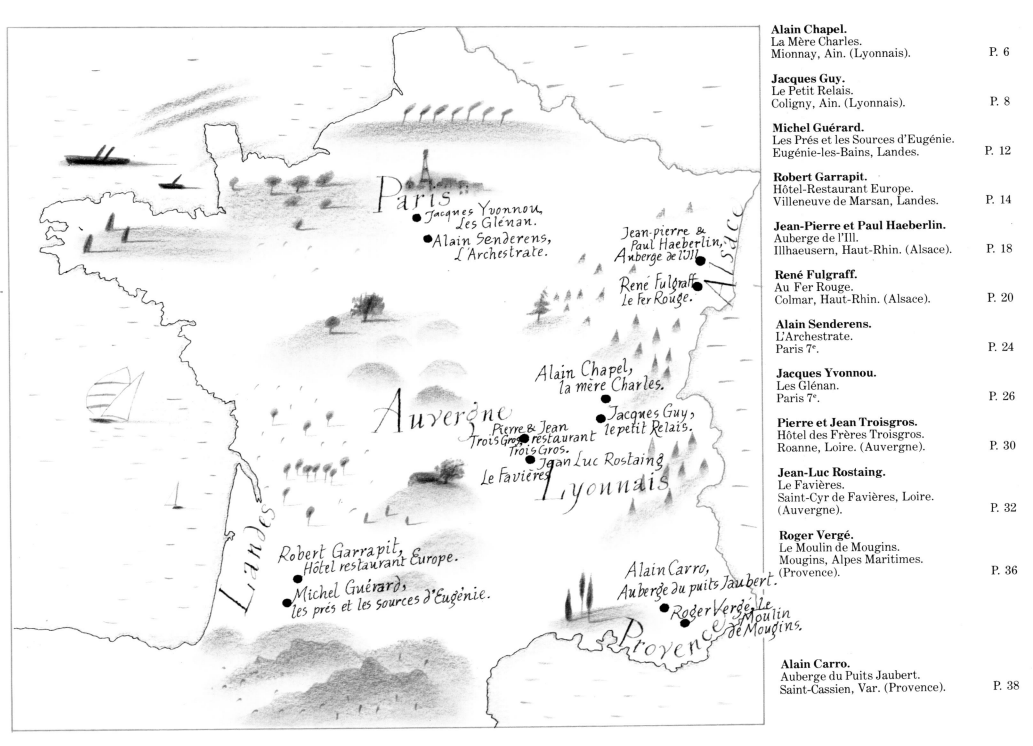

Paris

Jacques Yvonnou,
Les Glénan.

Alain Senderens,
L'Archestrate.

Jean-pierre &
Paul Haeberlin,
Auberge de l'Ill.

René Fulgraff.
Le Fer Rouge.

Auvergne

Alain Chapel,
la mère Charles.

Jacques Guy,
le petit Relais.

Pierre & Jean
Trois Gros, restaurant
Trois Gros.

Jean Luc Rostaing
Le Favières

Lyonnais

Robert Garrapit,
Hôtel restaurant Europe.

Michel Guérard,
les prés et les sources d'Eugénie.

Alain Carro,
Auberge du puits Jaubert.

Roger Vergé, Le
Moulin
de Mougins.

Provence

Landes

Alsace

Conversion table for British measures

The measurements used in this book are American cups/tablespoons followed by metric measures in parentheses. Since American and British measures differ, the following table will enable British users to convert from either of these systems.

1 cup = 16 tablespoons = 8 fluid ounces (approx. 0,8 pint)
1 tablespoon = 3 teaspoons = 1/2 fluid ounce.

1 litre = 35 fluid ounces (approx. 2 pints)
1/2 litre = 17 1/2 fluid ounces (approx. 1 pint)
250 ml = 8 3/4 fluid ounces (approx. 1/2 pint)
100 ml = 3 1/2 fluid ounces.

1 kg = 2 lb 3 oz (approx. 2 1/4 lb)
500 g = 1 lb 1 1/2 oz (approx. 1 lb)
250 g = 9 oz (approx. 1/2 lb)
125 g = 4 1/2 oz (approx. 1/4 lb)
100 g = 3 1/2 oz
28.35 g (approx. 30 g) = 1 oz.

Hors d'Oeuvres and Entrées.

Shellfish.

Fish.

Meat, Game and Poultry.

Desserts.

Cocktails.

Conceived and compiled by Doyle Dane Bernbach

Printed in France by the Imprimerie de Montreuil
Dépôt légal n° 78-3393, 3ᵉ trimestre 1978
ISBN n° 2-9500277-1-7

Published by SEGM / Division Ricard International - 2, rue de Solférino, 75007 Paris - SIRET 302 453 592 000 16 - R.C. Paris 74 B 5977 - S.A. au capital de 30 000 000 F